MIND THE GAP

MICHELLE MINTON

HOW IS DEVELOPMENT CHANGING IN SOUTHEAST ASIA AND BEYOND?

KS3 GEOGRAPHY TEACHERS' TOOLKIT

EDITED BY ALAN KINDER AND JOHN WIDDOWSON

Geographical Association

Online resources

Accompanying this book is a set of downloadable resources, such as activity sheets, images and background information.

To download your resources, visit *www.geography.org.uk/ks3toolkit* and click on the button for this book. You will then be asked for your password. The unique password for this book is **K3T41MM**.

ISBN 978-1-84377-374-0
First published 2016
Impression number 10 9 8 7 6 5 4 3 2 1
Year 2019 2018 2017

Published by the Geographical Association, 160 Solly Street, Sheffield S1 4BF
Company number: 07139068
Website: www.geography.org.uk
Email: info@geography.org.uk
The Geographical Association is a registered charity: no 1135148

The GA would be happy to hear from other potential authors who have ideas for geography books. You may contact the Publications Officer via the GA at the address above.

Copyedited by Fran Royle
Designed by Bryan Ledgard
Cartography by Paul Coles
Printed and bound in the UK by Lion FPG

Acknowledgements

Thanks to John Widdowson and Alan Kinder for their input and support throughout this project; to The Trailblazer Foundation for agreeing to be the case study used in lesson 8; and to Anna Grandfield and Bryan Ledgard for their presentation of this book.

CONTENTS

EDITORS' PREFACE

The *Key Stage 3 Geography Teachers' Toolkit* series is designed to help teachers create an exciting and challenging curriculum for their students by building geographical knowledge, ideas and skills into the exploration of important places, themes and issues around the world. The series provides guidance to teachers of geography to help them manage each new curriculum challenge with confidence.

We are delighted to be undertaking a major expansion of this award-winning series. The world around us is ever-changing; so too are the demands of the geography curriculum! The first new additions explore the emerging economies of Asia, delve deep into the geology of Britain, visit remote and extreme glacial environments and enquire into the way in which human use of resources places an increasing strain on our planet. The second new additions examine international development, in particular the causes and consequences of rapid development in Southeast Asia, and explore extreme weather and climate around the world.

Each title in the series, written by outstanding teachers of geography, provides a complete unit of work: a bank of ready-made lesson plans with downloadable activities and resources to bring the real world into your classroom.

For busy teachers of geography, each *Toolkit* provides material for immediate and direct use with students and involves minimal preparation. Materials can also be adapted and extended. Each book explains how teaching strategies have been applied to a particular curriculum context, providing a rich source of teacher-to-teacher advice. Links to further resources and reading offer opportunities to challenge even the highest-attaining students.

The series also provides a template for writing new curriculum materials. Unit summaries, curriculum maps linked to geographical knowledge, processes and skills, assessment frameworks, glossaries, lesson plans and other materials are included as exemplars of rigorous curriculum planning. By using tools from the kit, we hope all teachers will gain the confidence to develop ideas and shape a curriculum to meet the needs and interests of their own students.

Alan Kinder and John Widdowson, 2016.

WHY TEACH ABOUT DEVELOPMENT?

A new era of development

Our students are growing up in a changing world. The study of international development helps unravel some of its complexities, applying geographical theory to the real world. This Toolkit aims to open the minds of young people, to give them the confidence to challenge ideas about development and make sense of the complex world they live in. The once-clear division between more developed and less developed countries is becoming blurred. Many, previously less developed, countries are now classified as newly industrialised countries (NICs). We can celebrate the great gains in development over the last decades: the number of people living in extreme poverty has more than halved; more girls are in school than ever before and 2.1 billion more people have access to sanitation. However, in 2015 the gap between the richest and poorest widened to the extent that the richest 1 per cent of the world's population possess more wealth than the other 99 per cent combined (Hardoon *et al.*, 2016), and this gap looks set to widen further. These statistics demonstrate the complex issues of equality and justice we face.

Making connections

International development is a broad and far-reaching area of study, allowing for the exploration of a variety of geographical skills and ideas. This Toolkit encourages students to explore the interdependent nature of human and physical geography with a backdrop of real place knowledge. In doing so, it fulfils the requirements of the key stage 3 National Curriculum for students to 'understand how geographical processes interact to create distinctive human and physical landscapes which change over time'. The use of globes, maps, atlases, presentation of data and virtual fieldwork respond to the National Curriculum emphasis on the importance of developing geographical skills and fieldwork. The term 'international development' suggests the use of a global lens, but this Toolkit will also 'zoom in', encouraging students to apply their knowledge to development in Southeast Asia and compare and contrast development between and within countries in that region.

Questioning values and attitudes

The study of international development provides a platform for encouraging students to explore their own perspectives and moral values, and question – and perhaps challenge – them. Schools refer to their responsibility to cover these topics in a variety of ways: Personal, Social, Health and Economic Education (PSHEE), Citizenship, Global learning, Moral education, etc. The study of international development can help prepare young people to become informed and active global citizens. Therefore, this Toolkit aims to give teachers the confidence to tackle controversial issues and help them challenge common misconceptions, at the same time giving students the opportunity to critically reflect upon their own views and to consider positive action. Throughout the Toolkit there will be opportunities to assess student progress.

Full of Eastern Promise

It is vital that students have the opportunity to apply their understanding to a real world example. This Toolkit zooms in on the emerging economies of Southeast Asia; a region of the world that has previously been a 'black hole' in geography education, rarely visited in lessons. However, with its exponential economic growth, diverse culture, growing role in global manufacturing and rising popularity as a tourist destination, Southeast Asia is an ideal location for an in-depth case study of international development.

Reference

Hardoon, D., Fuentes-Nieva, R. and Ayele, S. (2016) *An Economy for the 1%: How privilege and power in the economy drive extreme inequality and how this can be stopped*. Oxford: Oxfam International.

HOW TO TEACH ABOUT DEVELOPMENT

Teaching a complex, far-reaching and ever-changing topic such as international development to key stage 3 students can be daunting for any teacher. Can or should this topic be simplified? Which named places and examples should we use? How can we make comparisons but avoid stereotypes? This Toolkit aims to address these issues and provide teachers with coherent guidance and an adaptable framework for introducing students to international development.

Defining development

Development is a debated topic amongst geographers. In this Toolkit, development is defined as 'the use of human and physical resources to improve standards of living'. 'Human resources' include such things as education, finance, labour, infrastructure and communications; 'physical resources' include things such as raw materials (minerals, oil, etc.), land and location. 'Standard of living' refers to factors such as healthcare provision, employment opportunities, sustainability, freedom of speech and gender equality.

A country's level of development can be measured by a set of statistics called development indicators, and in the past these were usually based on economic factors, using indicators such as gross domestic product (GDP). Now, however, a more holistic approach is favoured, taking account of social, economic and environmental development. For example, the United Nations Human Development Index (HDI) uses health, education and standard of living to rank countries in terms of development, scoring them to three decimal places from 0 (very low development) to 1 (very high development). In this Toolkit we use the terms 'more developed country' (MDC) and 'less developed country' (LDC) to refer to countries at different stages of development. The term 'newly industrialised country' (NIC) is also introduced. Although there is no consensus about the best terminology to use, we have opted for these descriptions; they could be debated and refined at a later stage, when and if students progress to GCSE and A level.

The wider topic of international development is concerned with development on a global scale and is the basis for international classifications, including those described above.

Challenging misconceptions

I'm sure you can already predict many student misconceptions about 'developed' and 'developing' countries before they arise in the classroom. Figure 1 shows some examples of stereotypical views from year 9 students.

'Poverty'
'Treehouses and mud huts'
'Children with no education'

Figure 1: Stereotypical views at year 9.

Students may have been exposed from a young age to a number of stereotypes or misconceptions reinforced by the media, family and friends; even, in some cases, schools. Such deeply embedded ideas are, by their nature, difficult to challenge and change. Below are my top tips for challenging student misconceptions and avoiding reinforcing them.

- Carefully consider the resources you use in the classroom (text, photographs, statistics, video clips). Do they support misconceptions/stereotypes? Whose voices are heard? Whose are missing?
- Be prepared before the lesson. Predict misconceptions that could arise in the context and be ready to respond to them with up-to-date factual information
- Help students develop the skills (e.g. media literacy) to critique sources of information and give them opportunities to practise them
- Give students tasks that surprise them and challenge their preconceptions; then allow them time for reflection
- Never ignore misconceptions/generalisations: openly discuss and address them
- Invite students to think about where they acquired their perceptions, and consider the reliability of these sources.

Tackling controversial issues

Controversial issues are described by Stradling (1985) as 'those... on which our society is clearly divided'. Debating them can cause conflict, but by addressing controversial issues in the classroom students can be encouraged to explore a range of perspectives, reflect upon their own views and develop confidence in public speaking. The topic of international development can trigger a range of controversial issues, such as:

- human factors affecting development (colonialism, governance, trade, power)
- the role of aid and charitable giving
- absolute and relative poverty
- immigration
- climate change.

Below are some recommendations to prepare you, and give you sufficient confidence, to address controversial issues and topics in the classroom.

- Develop a relationship with students that allows them to express their views openly, but address stereotypes and prejudices if they arise
- Use questioning techniques to facilitate discussions, rather than lead them; considering the opinions of others will help students reflect upon their own views
- Develop confidence in the topic by ensuring your understanding of it is up to date and appropriate
- Steer clear of prejudices and stereotypes by avoiding generalisations and weighted terminology
- Provide a historical context for the issue to ensure students appreciate the whole story
- Use a range of teaching strategies and resources, e.g. video, music, poetry, drama, personal learning and thinking skills (PLTS), to ensure the topic is accessible to all students.

Keep it up to date

One of the biggest difficulties when teaching about international development is keeping it up to date. Hans Rosling famously pointed out the ignorance of many adults when it comes to international development, with most people viewing the world as it was in the mid-1900s and even using loaded terms like 'first world' and 'third world'. His most recent videos – 'Don't Panic' and 'The River of Myths' (*www.gapminder.org/videos*) – emphasise the importance of real-time, accurate statistics, which are crucial for accurate and geographically grounded teaching about international development. Keeping it current also makes it real to students and can encourage them to engage with current affairs and geography in the news (see page 39 for a list of useful websites with up-to-date information and facts).

Using images

Images can be used in the geography classroom for a variety of purposes: to challenge misconceptions, develop critical thinking skills, build students' geographical imaginations, stimulate discussion and elicit emotional responses. All of these are relevant for the study of international development.

Below is a list of ways in which photographs could be used in the classroom to enhance teaching about international development (adapted from Leeds DEC, 2012).

Cropping: cover one or several parts of a photo and ask students to guess what the missing sections of the photo show, e.g. that wealthy and deprived areas can be located side by side.

Captions: give small groups or pairs of students a selection of photos, for which they must write both positive and negative captions, with reasons. This can raise their awareness of how they can be influenced in newspapers or magazines by the way images are captioned.

Feelings: show students a range of photos from different parts of the world. How does this photo make them feel? Why?

Sorting into sets: ask groups of students to sort pictures into sets. You can let them choose the categories. If they found any pictures difficult to categorise, ask them to explain why.

Sequencing: give groups of students six or seven pictures that have some connection with each other. Ask them to use them to tell a story, putting the photographs in whatever order they decide. This could lead to a discussion about why some countries are poor, or about different approaches to development.

Speech bubbles: give students a set of photographs and some speech bubbles and ask them to write what the people in the photographs might be saying.

Ranking: give pairs or groups of students six photographs and ask them to arrange them in a triangle, with one at the top and three at the bottom, ranking them according to such criteria as development, quality of life, and standard of living.

Summary

In this unit students will investigate development at a variety of scales. They will critically consider what development means for people and places, how development can be measured, where the most and least developed places are in the world, why development is unequal and who is responsible for generating development. They will also take a closer look at present and potential future development in Southeast Asia. Each lesson starts with an enquiry question, learning objective(s) and differentiated learning outcomes, which should be re-visited at the end of the lesson so both teachers and students can assess their progress.

Prior learning

In key stage 2 students should have begun to study the following in relation to this topic: trade links; the distribution of natural resources, including energy, food, minerals and water; and economic activity. They should also have some understanding of similarities and differences between the United Kingdom, a region in a European country and a region in North or South America.

Future learning

By the end of this topic students should have a better understanding and knowledge of the geography of development, including measuring development, explaining differences in development around the world and within Southeast Asia, and different approaches to development. These lessons and case studies provide a solid foundation for the study of development theories, barriers to development and sustainable development at GCSE.

Key learning outcomes

Most students will be able to:

- define 'development' and apply the terms MDC, LDC and NIC to different countries using development indicators
- explain the factors that can influence development around the world and within a country, giving examples
- explain the costs and benefits of large-scale and small-scale approaches to development
- describe and begin to explain the costs and benefits of the Millennium Development Goals and global approaches to development in general
- Explain the roles of different stakeholders in development, using examples
- Interpret atlas maps, graphs and development indicators to explain the development of different countries.

Some students will not have made so much progress and will be able to:

- show some understanding of the term 'development' and describe ways it can be measured
- describe simply how a number of factors can influence development around the world
- identify and describe differences between small- and large-scale approaches to development
- name a range of Millennium Development Goals and describe their role
- identify and begin to describe the role of different stakeholders in development
- use atlas maps to identify countries and major cities.

Some students will have progressed further and will be able to:

- assess countries' development, using a range of development indicators
- explore links between factors influencing development around the world and within countries
- evaluate large- and small-scale approaches to development, giving named examples as evidence
- evaluate the success of the Millennium Development Goals, giving evidence
- assess the responsibility of different stakeholders in development, and explore their own role in development
- use a wide range of resources, including atlas maps, graphs, development indicators and choropleth maps, to research the current and potential future development of different countries.

THE GEOGRAPHY OF DEVELOPMENT

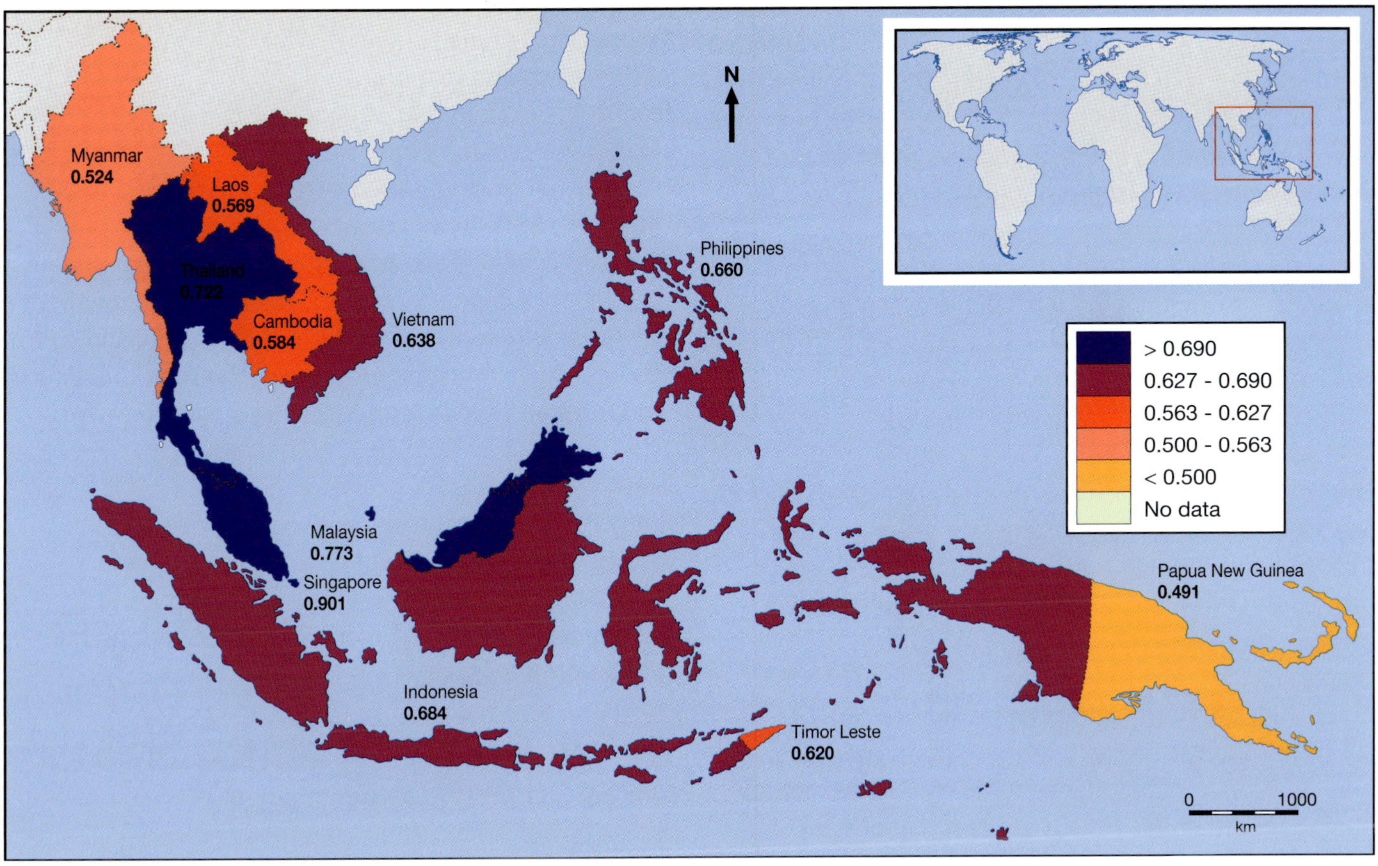

Figure 2: HDI levels worldwide in 1995. Source: http://hdr.undp.org/en/data/map.

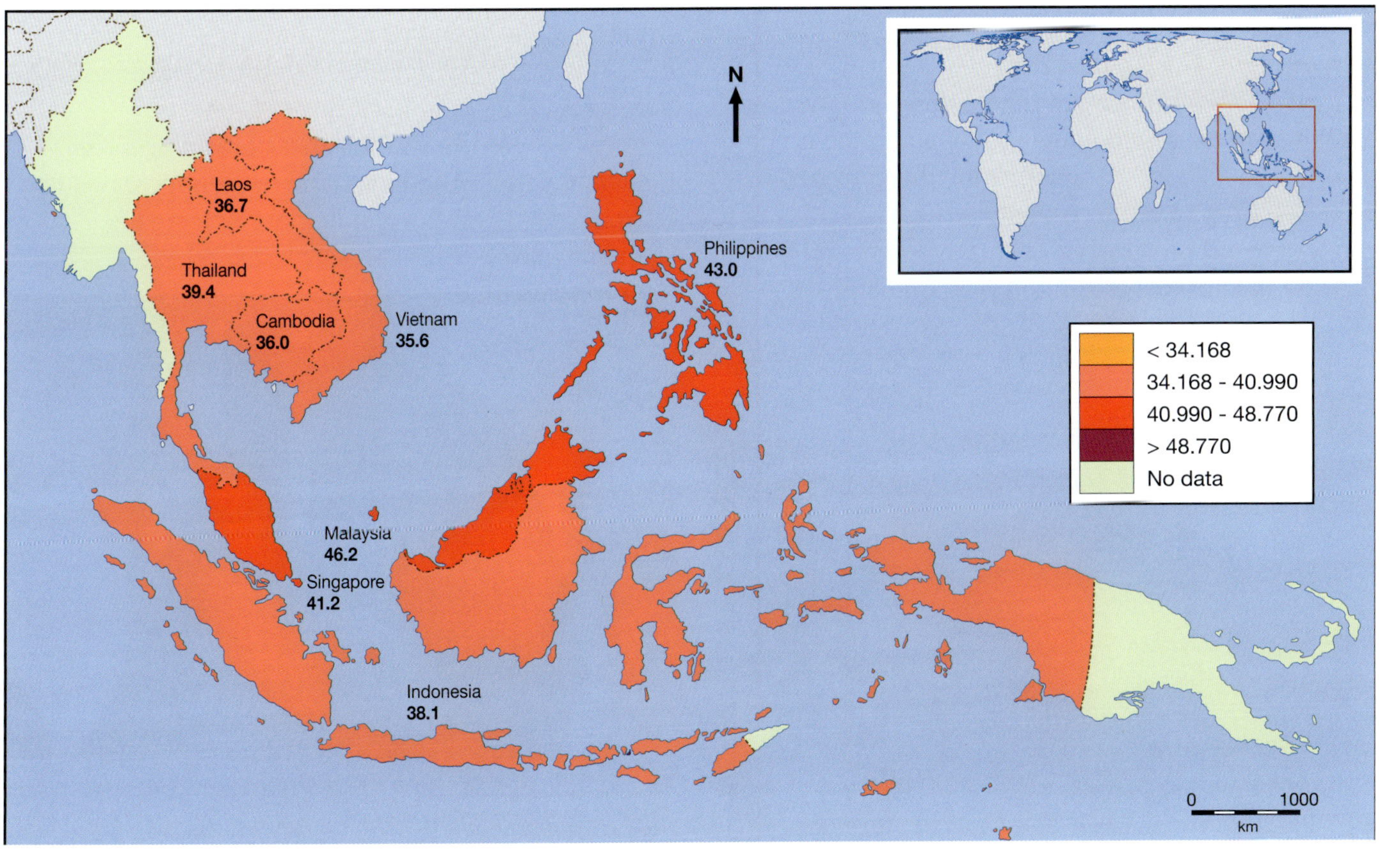

Figure 3: HDI levels worldwide in 2013. Source: http://hdr.undp.org/en/data/map.

Development around the world

Figures 2 and 3 show the UN Human Development Index (HDI) levels of countries in 1995 and 2013. It is clear that Asia has seen rapid gains over the last 20 years, but why have some countries and regions 'developed' faster than others? Some of the factors are highlighted below.

Population

A large or growing population has the potential to generate an important skills base; however, it can also put a strain on public services and resources.

Natural resources

Countries/regions with significant natural resources, e.g. oil, diamonds or cocoa, can generate income to fund development through trade, especially if they also process the raw materials into manufactured goods.

Geographic location

Access to trade routes and close proximity to other countries increases opportunities to trade goods and help develop a country. Geographically isolated regions (due to mountainous terrain or island nations, for example) can suffer from a lack of markets/investment for trade or difficulty in developing infrastructure.

Governance and conflict

In some countries, poor governance and corruption can lead to a lack of development. National income is allocated to military spending, rather than invested in public services. In war-torn countries high casualty rates can lead to a shortage of working-age people and an increase in dependents (e.g. refugees, orphans).

Photo © The Stimson Center.

An example of a 'top down' development: Xayaburi Hydroelectric Dam, Laos.

Colonialism

Colonialism can be beneficial, fostering trade partnerships and manufacturing growth, but it can also lead to the exploitation of people and resources, hindering development.

HIV/AIDS

This largely affects the working-age population; unable to work, they cannot contribute to economic growth or pay taxes. Often, orphan children cannot afford to go to school, which limits their future contribution to a skilled workforce and the country's economic development.

Tourism

Countries with spectacular scenery or a rich cultural history can earn significant revenue from tourism. However, tourism is not always a reliable source of income and can cause environmental degradation or intercultural tension.

Development in Southeast Asia

Why has Southeast Asia's development been so rapid in recent times? Globalisation and the growth of TNCs (transnational corporations) have had a major role to play. Southeast Asia offers TNCs a large, skilled workforce, low operating costs and a well-developed infrastructure. More developed countries have outsourced their manufacturing (e.g. textiles, automotive, electronics industries), providing direct foreign investment and jobs. The result is increased tax revenue and a growing middle class with greater spending power.

Photo © Michelle Minton.

An example of a 'bottom up' development: Bio-sand water filter installed in Siem Reap, Cambodia, by the Trailblazer Foundation.

However, development remains unequal, both between and within countries. Singapore has the highest HDI in Southeast Asia, with a score of 0.901 (the 9th highest in the world), whereas Myanmar (formerly Burma) has the lowest in this region at 0.524 (150th in the world). There is a wide disparity between rural and urban regions, which generally have better education, healthcare and sanitation; this results in rural to urban migration. However, cities also show disparities; for example, the population of Manila in the Philippines includes millionaires but also two million people living in slum housing.

Approaches to development

Large-scale development projects are usually expensive, funded by governments, TNCs or global institutions (e.g. the World Bank) and managed from the 'top down'. Conversely, small-scale approaches are usually cheap, funded and managed at a community level by non-governmental organisations (NGOs), charities, etc., and decision making is from the 'bottom up'. Both approaches have advantages and disadvantages and it is too simplistic to conclude one approach is always better than the other.

The Global Goals for Sustainable Development

In 2015, world leaders at the United Nations committed the world to achieving 17 Global Goals (see Figure 6) by 2030. These follow on from the Millennium Development Goals (MDGs) that were set in 2000, which aimed to close the 'development gap' within 15 years, and range from eradicating poverty to creating sustainable cities and achieving peace and justice. Critics of the MDGs believed some of the goals were unattainable, too simplistic, ignored the need for wealthier countries to improve sustainability, and lacked engagement with less developed countries. However, supporters of the MDGs celebrate their successes: for example, 74 countries halved their levels of poverty and 2.3 billion more people gained access to clean water.

Figure 6: The 17 Global Goals, 2015.

CONCEPTS AND CURRICULUM LINKS

In key stage 3 geography students should be taught locational knowledge, place knowledge, human and physical geography (including how human and physical processes interact with the environment) plus geographical skills and fieldwork.

I have used these areas of geography to create a curriculum map for this book. The map lists the key questions that are the basis of enquiry in all the lessons.

As you might expect in a book about development, there are many links between human, environmental and physical geography. Creating a curriculum map (see Figure 7) helps to ensure we teach a broad and balanced curriculum.

Development in the 21st Century

1. Introducing Development

What is development?

How can development be measured?

2. Investigating global development

How does development vary around the world?

Why does wealth vary around the world?

3. Zooming in on Southeast Asia

How and why has Southeast Asia's development changed over time?

How equal is development in Southeast Asia?

4. Making development happen

What is the difference between large-scale and small-scale development?

How effective are large- and small-scale approaches to development?

How can countries work together to support development?

Figure 7: Plotting your broad and balanced geography curriculum in map form.

New Oxfam report says half of global wealth held by 1%

By **Larry Elliott**, *economics editor, and* **Ed Pilkington**, *chief reporter for* Guardian US.

Billionaires and politicians gathering in Switzerland this week will come under pressure to tackle rising inequality after a study found that – on current trends – by next year, 1% of the world's population will own more wealth than the other 99%.

Ahead of this week's annual meeting of the World Economic Forum in the ski resort of Davos, the anti-poverty charity Oxfam said it would use its high-profile role at the gathering to demand urgent action to narrow the gap between rich and poor.

The charity's research, published on Monday, shows that the share of the world's wealth owned by the best-off 1% has increased from 44% in 2009 to 48% in 2014, while the least well-off 80% currently own just 5.5%.

Oxfam added that on current trends the richest 1% would own more than 50% of the world's wealth by 2016.

Winnie Byanyima, executive director of Oxfam International and one of the six co-chairs at this year's WEF, said the increased concentration of wealth seen since the deep recession of 2008-09 was dangerous and needed to be reversed.

In an interview with the *Guardian*, Byanyima said: 'We want to bring a message from the people in the poorest countries in the world to the forum of the most powerful business and political leaders.

'The message is that rising inequality is dangerous. It's bad for growth and it's bad for governance. We see a concentration of wealth capturing power and leaving ordinary people voiceless and their interests uncared for.'

Oxfam made headlines at Davos last year with a study showing that the 85 richest people on the planet have the same wealth as the poorest 50% (3.5 billion people). The charity said this year that the comparison was now even more stark, with just 80 people owning the same amount of wealth as more than 3.5 billion people, down from 388 in 2010.

Byanyima said: 'Do we really want to live in a world where the 1% own more than the rest of us combined? The scale of global inequality is quite simply staggering and despite the issues shooting up the global agenda, the gap between the richest and the rest is widening fast.'

Separate research by the Equality Trust, which campaigns to reduce inequality in the UK, found that the richest 100 families in Britain in 2008 had seen their combined wealth increase by at least £15bn, a period during which average income increased by £1,233. Britain's current richest 100 had the same wealth as 30% of UK households, it added.

Oxfam said it was calling on governments to adopt a seven point plan:

- Clamp down on tax dodging by corporations and rich individuals.
- Invest in universal, free public services such as health and education.
- Share the tax burden fairly, shifting taxation from labour and consumption towards capital and wealth.
- Introduce minimum wages and move towards a living wage for all workers.
- Introduce equal pay legislation and promote economic policies to give women a fair deal.
- Ensure adequate safety-nets for the poorest, including a minimum-income guarantee.
- Agree a global goal to tackle inequality.

Speaking to the *Guardian*, Byanyima added: 'Extreme inequality is not just an accident or a natural rule of economics. It is the result of policies and with different policies it can be reduced. I am optimistic that there will be change'.

Source: Elliott, L. and Pilkington, E. (2015) New Oxfam report says half of global wealth held by the 1%, Available at: www.theguardian.com/business/2015/jan/19/global-wealth-oxfam-inequality-davos-economic-summit-switzerland (last accessed 3/3/2016).

Photo © David McIntyre Crossroads Foundation Ltd.

MEDIUM-TERM PLAN

Lesson	Key questions	Learning objectives	Teaching and learning	Resources	Assessment opportunities
1. Defining develop-ment	What is development?	To define the term 'development' To explore the complexity of the term 'development'	**Starter**: Students complete a baseline questionnaire to establish current understanding of development **Main**: Students complete a 'mind movie' exercise to consider what a perfect 'developed' world would look like and define the term development. Students categorise facts and photographs into Less Developed Countries (LDCs) and More Developed Countries (MDCs) **Plenary**: Students stand on a 'geography continuum' to show how much they agree with the statement 'all countries with lots of money are MDCs'	Activity Sheets 1, 2 and 3 PowerPoint 1	Students define the term 'development' Students categorise countries as MDC or LDC and justify their choices Students explain why 'development' is a difficult concept to define
2. Measuring develop-ment	How can development be measured?	To understand and evaluate a range of development indicators	**Starter**: Students undertake an intelligent guesswork activity to predict global statistics **Main**: Students match development indicators to their definitions and then apply their understanding to three geographical research questions **Plenary**: Students complete a diamond 9 exercise to decide on the best way to measure development and justify their decisions	Activity Sheets 4 and 5 Glue Information Sheet 1 Internet access PowerPoint 2 Scissors	Students match development indicators to their definitions Students allocate development indicators to different questions and explain their choices Students rank the effectiveness of each development indicator and justify their choices
3. Varying develop-ment	How does development vary around the world?	To investigate how different countries' development varies around the world To use data to create an accurate choropleth map	**Starter**: Students receive a Top Trumps card and predict their place on a continuum to show the development of countries from LDC to MDC **Main**: Students play Top Trumps using development indicators to discover how development varies between countries. The Human Development Index (HDI) is explained and students construct a choropleth map to show the level of development of different countries **Plenary**: Students use choropleth maps to describe and explain how development varies around the world	Activity Sheets 6 and 7 Atlases PowerPoint 3	Student contribution to class discussion Students construct a choropleth map and analyse it

Lesson	Key questions	Learning objectives	Teaching and learning	Resources	Assessment opportunities
4. Development Factors	Why does wealth vary around the world?	To investigate factors that can affect wealth and development around the world	**Starter**: Students work in groups to organise reasons why some people and places in the world are poorer than others, in whichever way they choose **Main**: Students travel around the classroom information display to research why some people and places in the world are poorer than others, note-taking as they do **Plenary**: Students return to their groups and add more reasons and information to create a concept map to answer the original enquiry question	A3 paper Information Sheets 2-6 PowerPoint 4 Sticky notes	Students create a group concept map to explain the factors that influence development around the world
5. Changing development	How has Southeast Asia's development changed over time, and why?	To investigate how and why Southeast Asia's development has changed over time	**Starter**: As statements are revealed one at a time, students try to guess the case study location for this lesson **Main**: Students carry out *Gapminder* research into development in Southeast Asia, share their findings, and attempt to explain the recent and rapid development **Plenary**: Students write and present a short news item summarising development in Southeast Asia using differentiated success criteria	Activity Sheet 8 Information Sheet 7 PowerPoint 5 *www.gapminder.org*	Students describe and explain how development in Southeast Asia has changed over time in a short news item
6. Equal development?	How equal is development in Southeast Asia?	To investigate how development varies across Southeast Asia	**Starter**: Students use an atlas to find the location of their allocated role play character from Southeast Asia. **Main**: Students write a diary entry based on their character, their family and social life, livelihood, challenges they face, achievements and how they feel. During the lesson newsflashes appear and change the life of each character; students respond to this in their diary entry **Plenary**: Students use statistics to explore the varied development across Southeast Asia and answer the following questions: How equal is development throughout Southeast Asia? Why does development vary throughout Southeast Asia?	Activity Sheets 9 and 10 Atlases PowerPoint 6	Students write diary entries to describe and explain the lifestyles of people in different income groups across Southeast Asia Students summarise how equal they believe development is throughout Southeast Asia and why inequalities exist

Lesson	Key questions	Learning objectives	Teaching and learning	Resources	Assessment opportunities
7. The scale of develop-ment	What is the difference between large-scale and small-scale development? How effective are large-scale approaches to development?	To explore the roles of large-scale and small-scale approaches to development	**Starter**: Students look at two photographs and attempt to spot the differences between a large-scale and a small-scale development project **Main**: Using a newspaper article about the Xayaburi Dam in Laos, students use five 'thinking hats' to investigate large-scale approaches to development. What and where is the Xayaburi Dam? What do different people feel about the Xayaburi Dam? What are the benefits of the Xayaburi Dam? What are the disadvantages of the Xayaburi Dam? What new ideas or alternatives are there to solve issues or costs of the Xayaburi Dam? Students then play 'argument tennis' in pairs using the costs and benefits of large-scale approaches to development they have just learnt about **Plenary**: As a whole class, students discuss all the 'ace' points from their argument tennis and see if others have a 'return'	Activity Sheet 11 Information Sheets 8 and 9 PowerPoint 7	Students use geographical thinking hats to evaluate the Xayaburi Dam project Students play 'argument tennis' to demonstrate the advantages and disadvantages of a large-scale approach to development
8. Cost-effective develop-ment?	How effective are small-scale development projects?	To explore the role of small-scale development projects	**Starter**: Students brainstorm all the ways they have used water since the beginning of the day **Main**: Five students become actors and take on the roles of five stakeholders involved with the Trailblazer Foundation, an NGO working in Siem Reap, Cambodia. The rest of the class ask the actors questions to discover the impacts of small-scale approaches to development **Plenary**: Students evaluate small- and large-scale approaches to development by completing a cost-benefit analysis	Activity Sheets 12, 13, 14 and 15 PowerPoint 8	Students evaluate small- and large-scale approaches to development by carrying out a cost-benefit analysis
9. Supporting develop-ment	How can countries work together to support development?	To explore global approaches to development	**Starter**: Students set themselves three SMART (specific, measurable, achievable, relevant and timely) goals linked to their lives **Main**: In pairs, students sort cards, which include statements reflecting the impacts of the Millennium	Activity Sheet 16 PowerPoint 9	Students write a PEE chain paragraph to explain why they think the MDGs have been successful or not Students work in groups of four to write

Lesson	Key questions	Learning objectives	Teaching and learning	Resources	Assessment opportunities
			Development Goals (MDGs), into categories. Students then write a PEE (point, evidence, explain) chain paragraph to explain whether they believe the MDGs were successful **Plenary**: In groups students choose and advocate new global development goals, then the class vote on the three they believe are most important and compare them to the new Global Goals		a campaign speech advocating a new goal for global development
10. Develop-ment roles	Whose responsibility is development and do we have a role to play?	To investigate the role of different stakeholders in development	**Starter**: Students study photographs and consider who is responsible for each of the situations shown **Main**: Students read statements relating to the impact eight different stakeholders can have on development. In pairs, students decide who they believe holds the greatest responsibility for development and justify their answer. Students return to their photograph from the starter and consider the role they could play in the situation shown **Plenary**: Students write a 'citizenship charter' suggesting how individuals can support development in the UK and around the world. Students also complete a questionnaire for comparison with the baseline questionnaire from the beginning of the unit	Activity Sheets 17, 18 and 19 PowerPoint 10	Students discuss the responsibility of different stakeholders in development Students write a citizenship charter that consolidates understanding from this unit of work A comparison of students' answers to the baseline questionnaire and the progress questionnaire

LESSON 1: Defining development

Key questions
- What is development?

Learning objectives
- To define the term 'development'
- To explore the complexity of the term 'development'

Key words
- Development
- More developed country (MDC)
- Less developed country (LDC)
- Newly industrialised country (NIC)

Resources
- Activity Sheet 1: Baseline questionnaire – What do you think about international development?
- Activity Sheet 2: My perfect world
- Activity Sheet 3: More developed country or less developed country?
- PowerPoint 1

Assessment opportunities
- Students define the term 'development'
- Students categorise countries as MDC or LDC and justify their choices
- Students explain why 'development' is a difficult concept to define

Starter
Use **Activity Sheet 1** to help establish what students already think and know about wealth and poverty internationally. This questionnaire can be used at the end of the unit to measure attitudinal change and student progress.

Main teaching phase

Mind Movie activity

Ask students to close their eyes while you read out the script from Figure 8 to them.

Hand out **Activity Sheet 2** and ask students to complete each of the four boxes to describe what their perfect world would look like. Students should share their visions for a perfect world with their partner and then with the rest of the class. Do we currently live in a perfect world? Which parts of our world are not perfect?

> As you close your eyes I would like you to think about the world we live in. First, think about your local area – the street you live on, your school and your local community. What problems do people face in your local area? What problems do you face? Now, think about the rest of this country – what do you think are the main problems facing the country? Think about problems facing people and the environment. Finally, broaden your thinking to the whole world – where in the world is suffering? What problems are people facing? Where is the environment being damaged? Now, imagine that tonight when you go to sleep something magical will happen... when you wake up in the morning the world you live in will be perfect... your local community will be perfect, the whole of this country will be perfect, and the rest of the world will be perfect. Hold onto this view of the world and open your eyes without speaking to anyone.

Figure 8: Text to read out for the Mind Movie activity.

Is this the same all over the world? Where is the most 'perfect' place on Earth to live today? Why? Can our world ever be perfect? Why? Why not?

Defining development

Students use **PowerPoint 1**, **slide 2**, to 'crack the code' and find the definition of development: 'The use of human and physical resources to improve standards of living'. They add this definition to **Activity Sheet 2**.

You could make links between this definition and students' visions of a perfect world, which represent an improved standard of living. Will everyone around the world agree with this definition? Why? Why not? Will everyone have the same view of development? Will everyone's vision of a perfect world be the same? Why? Why not?

Tell students that while countries can be categorised as a high income country (HIC), medium income country (MIC) and low income country (LIC) when classified by wealth, they can also be categorised as more developed countries (MDCs) and less developed countries (LDCs). Hand out **Activity Sheet 3** and show students **PowerPoint 1**, **slides 4–6**. For each slide students should complete the table on **Activity Sheet 3** by

Photo © Tony Alter.

Photo © Byelikova Oksana/Shutterstock.

Photo © Nicolas Vollmer.

Photo © John Berns.

guessing the country described on each slide, categorising it as an MDC or LDC, and then justifying their choice using evidence from the slide. This activity aims to challenge students to appreciate a complex idea of MDC and LDCs and to demonstrate that it is not as simple to categorise a country's level of development as it may at first appear.

Use **PowerPoint 1**, **slide 7**, to share the answers. You could introduce the term newly industrialised country (NIC) here for Thailand, if appropriate for your class. During class discussions ask students to consider what they found difficult about this activity. Is it easy to decide whether a country is an MDC or LDC? Why? What did you have to consider when deciding if a country was an MDC or LDC? Why could the terms MDC and LDC be misleading?

Plenary

Show students **PowerPoint 1**, **slide 8**. Students should consider the statement 'All rich countries are MDCs'. Students could write their response to the statement on a mini-whiteboard. Students then stand along a continuum from one side of the classroom to the other to show the extent to which they agree or disagree with this statement. Use questioning here to listen to a range of opinions and give students the opportunity to reflect on their opinion and alter their place on the continuum. Students could then improve their previous definition of development from the crack the code activity to include the new terms (MDC, LDC and NIC) and demonstrate growing understanding of the complexity of the term 'development'.

Extension or homework activity

The UK is an MDC but it is far from perfect! Ask students to think of ten ways in which this country could be improved to make it a better place to live. They should give reasons for their ideas. This will help them to understand that development is a process that continues, even when a country is classified as an MDC.

Teaching tips

It is vital to use questioning throughout this topic to probe students' understanding and challenge common misconceptions and stereotypes about more developed and less developed countries. Increase the complexity and challenge of questioning as the lesson and unit progresses. Bloom's taxonomy is a useful starting point for personalised questioning (see **PowerPoint 1**, **slide 9**).

You could collate the information from **Activity Sheet 1** to influence future lesson planning. You could also revisit this with students at the end of the unit to help them reflect upon their learning over the course of the ten lessons and to measure progress and attitudinal change.

LESSON 2: Measuring development

Key question

- How can development be measured?

Learning objective

- To understand and evaluate a range of development indicators

Key words

- Development indicator
- Gross domestic product per capita (GDP/capita)
- Infant mortality rate
- Life expectancy
- Literacy rate
- Poverty line

Resources

- Activity Sheet 4: Development indicator card sort
- Activity Sheet 5: How can we measure a country's development?
- Glue
- Information Sheet 1: Development indicator card sort – Answers
- Internet access
- PowerPoint 2
- Scissors

Assessment opportunities

- Students match development indicators to their definitions
- Students allocate development indicators to different questions and explain their choices
- Students rank the effectiveness of each development indicator and justify their choices

Starter

Go to *www.worldometers.info*, preferably before the lesson, to find the latest figures for the data below.

Either show **PowerPoint 2**, **slide 2**, or write the following on the board:

- current world population
- cars produced this year
- emails sent today
- people who died of hunger today
- tons of carbon dioxide emissions produced this year.

Ask students which they think is the biggest number, and which is increasing at the fastest rate. To challenge more able students encourage them to justify their predictions on mini-whiteboards or in their exercise book.

Now, share the actual figures for the data with students. You can also visit the Worldometers website live to show a wide range of statistics, which are continuously updating. Ask:

- How do these figures compare to 100 years ago?
- How might these figures vary around the world?
- How do these figures relate to a country's development?

Main teaching phase

Development indicators match-up

Hand out **Activity Sheet 4** to students (you may like to have **Information Sheet 1: Answers** or the answers here to hand). Students cut along the dotted lines and match the development indicator card to the correct definition card. Once checked, students glue the definition cards into their exercise books with the development indicators on top, creating a flap, which, when lifted, reveals the correct definition. More able students, or those who finish first, should attempt to answer the 'challenges' on each of the cards.

Applying development indicators

Students must now apply their understanding of these development indicators. Using **Activity Sheet 5**, they should consider each of the questions (see also below) and decide which development indicators would help them answer it.

- How effective is the healthcare in a country?
- How equal is the development in a country?
- How environmentally sustainable is a country?

For example, life expectancy and infant mortality rate would help students to answer the first question. More able students should be encouraged to explain how the development indicators would help them answer the question. For example, if a country has high life expectancy, it is likely that it has high-quality, accessible healthcare and immunisation programmes.

	**Development indicator** Life expectancy	**Definition** The average age a person is likely to live until *Challenge:* What could this tell you about the quality of healthcare?
	**Development indicator** Gross domestic product per capita (GDP/C)	**Definition** The amount of money a country earns divided by the number of people who live there *Challenge:* What information does this indicator not tell you?
	**Development indicator** Literacy rate	**Definition** The percentage of people aged 15 and over who can read and write *Challenge:* How could this affect the type of jobs people could do?
	**Development indicator** Access to clean water	**Definition** The percentage of people who have access to clean water *Challenge:* How could this affect a country's life expectancy?
	**Development indicator** Percentage of population below the poverty line	**Definition** The percentage of people in a country who are living in poverty *Challenge:* Why does this vary around the world?
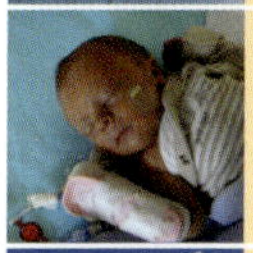	**Development indicator** Infant mortality rate	**Definition** The number of babies per 1000 born who die before their first birthday *Challenge:* Why could this be high in an LDC?
	**Development indicator** Number of internet users	**Definition** The number of people in a country who have access to the internet *Challenge:* How could internet access help a country's businesses?
	**Development indicator** Population change	**Definition** The percentage change in a population each year. This could be positive (a population increase) or negative (a population decrease) *Challenge:* What are the advantages and disadvantages of a large population?
	**Development indicator** Energy consumption	**Definition** A country's annual energy usage in kilowatts per hour (kWh) *Challenge:* How could this affect the environment?

Plenary

Having learnt and applied a variety of development indicators, students should now be able to consider how effective each is at measuring development. It might be useful at this point to refer back to the development definitions they wrote in the previous lesson. On **Activity Sheet 5** there is a diamond 9, which will help students rank the effectiveness of each development indicator. The following questions are included on the worksheet and can be used as part of a class discussion before the activity to get students thinking critically about each indicator.

- How important is this indicator for people's quality of life?
- What additional information about the development of a country could you infer from this indicator?
- What does this indicator miss out?
- How might this indicator vary across a country? For example, could there be differences between males and females, or between rural (countryside) and urban (city) areas?

More able students should justify their diamond 9 choices, demonstrating their evaluation of each development indicator.

Extension or homework activity

A suitable homework follow-up activity for this lesson could be to ask students to use the CIA World Factbook (*www.cia.gov/library/publications/the-world-factbook*) to research the development indicators for a specific country and present them in a fact file, with a paragraph describing the country's level of development. These could be displayed around a world map on the classroom wall, to support learning throughout this topic. Additionally, if there is an upcoming major event (e.g. FIFA World Cup, Olympic Games, Eurovision Song Contest) students could be allocated countries linked to the event to investigate how a country's level of development can influence its success in the event.

Teaching tip

This lesson uses intelligent guesswork, which promotes students' numeracy skills. This also provides an opportunity to discuss data reliability with students.

LESSON 3: Varying development

Key question

- How does development vary around the world?

Learning objectives

- To investigate how different countries' development varies around the world
- To use data to create an accurate choropleth map

Key words

- Choropleth map
- Human Development Index (HDI)

Resources

- Activity Sheet 6: Development Top Trumps cards
- Activity Sheet 7: World HDI choropleth map
- Atlases
- PowerPoint 3

Assessment opportunities

- Student contribution to class discussion
- Students construct a choropleth map and analyse it

Before the lesson

This lesson requires space for students to stand along a 'geography continuum' and move around the classroom, therefore classrooms may need preparing before the lesson begins.

Starter

Print out and cut up the Top Trumps cards (**Activity Sheet 6, page 1**) and give one to each pair of students. Each card carries the name of a country and a number of development indicators from the CIA World Factbook. Ask students to locate their country using an atlas and to label their card with the continent in which their country is located, and tell them that they have one minute to consider how developed their country is, using the development indicators on their card. Now explain to students that the next activity has to be completed in absolute silence. All pairs must arrange themselves along a geography continuum to indicate how developed their country is, from less developed countries (LDCs) to more developed countries (MDCs). They are not allowed to show other students their Top Trumps card and they must use other means to communicate (e.g. miming). Select some students to explain their position using the data on their Top Trumps card as evidence.

Main teaching phase

Development Top Trumps

In their pairs, students now play Top Trumps with other pairs (see Figure 9), rearranging themselves along the geography continuum. Once students appear confident with their position on the continuum, work from the MDC end and ask students to name their country and provide one reason for their place on the continuum, using data from their Top Trumps card. **PowerPoint 3, slide 2** has a sentence starter to support students with this verbal explanation. You may want to record the order of the countries on a whiteboard to refer back to later in the lesson. How accurate is their geography continuum? Have they encountered any difficulties deciding where they should stand? Do any pairs disagree with their position? Why? This questioning aims to draw out the downfalls of using just one indicator to measure development.

1. One pair chooses the development indicator they would like to 'play' and shares this indicator and figure with the other pair.
2. The pair with the highest number, which means it is more developed than the country it is playing against, wins.
3. Pairs who win should move towards the MDC end of the continuum, and pairs who lose move towards the LDC end of the continuum.
4. Students continue to play Top Trumps with other pairs to help them decide where they should be on the geography continuum.

Figure 9: Top Trumps rules.

Scoring development

Show students **PowerPoint 3**, **slide 3** and explain what the HDI is and how it is a more effective way to measure development. Depending on the ability of the class you may want to discuss the downfalls of the HDI (i.e. it doesn't reflect inequalities, human rights, sustainability, gender disparities). Looking at the data on slide 4, students note their country's HDI score on their card. Students should now rearrange themselves on the continuum using the HDI score for their country (scores are between 0 (LDC) and 1 (MDC), using three decimal places). The correct order is shown below. You may like to compare this continuum to the previous one. Who has moved? What are the benefits of using HDI to measure development?

Mapping development

Provide students with atlases and A3 copies of **Activity Sheet 7** and ask them to use the data in the table to complete a choropleth map. They choose four colours to complete the key and then use their atlases to locate and shade in each country in the table.

Plenary

Students use their choropleth map to describe and explain how development varies around the world, using HDI scores as evidence and inferring what this shows about each country's level of development. **PowerPoint 3**, **slide 5** includes a writing frame to support less able students. More able students should be encouraged to evaluate the use of the HDI to measure development. What does the HDI still miss out? What additional information would be useful to help understand the development of a region in more detail?

Extension or homework activity

You could build on this activity to explore patterns of development. Ask students to step forward to illustrate what continent they are in. Where are MDCs predominantly located? Why? Where are LDCs predominantly located? Why?

Teaching tip

Ask students to locate the country they have been given in an atlas. Regular use of this strategy reinforces their locational knowledge and atlas skills.

Continuum of the completed top trumps cards, based on the HDI score and running from LDC (Least) to MDC (Most).

LESSON 4: Development factors

Key question
- Why does wealth vary around the world?

Learning objective
- To investigate factors that can affect wealth and development around the world

Key words
- Accessibility
- Colonialism
- Conflict
- Infrastructure
- Topography
- Youthful population

Resources
- A3 paper (one piece per group of 3/4 students)
- Information Sheet 2: Bolivia – Population profile
- Information Sheet 3: India – Factors affecting development
- Information Sheet 4: Myanmar (Burma) – Topography and colonial past
- Information Sheet 5: DR Congo – Conflict, corruption and mineral wealth
- Information Sheet 6: South Africa – Sickness and safaris
- PowerPoint 4
- Sticky notes

Assessment opportunities
Students create a group concept map to explain the factors that influence development around the world

Starter
This lesson takes the form of an independent enquiry (Figure 10). Students are posed the enquiry question 'Why are some people and places in the world poorer than others?' They have to generate a hypothesis/ prediction, investigate the issue and reflect on the answer, and to start with they each write three possible reasons on three separate sticky notes. You could suggest some aspects here to guide them, e.g. natural hazards (drought, earthquakes), climate, debt, conflict, resources, colonialism, corruption, disease, etc. Now give groups of three or four students a piece of A3 paper and ask them to use it to arrange the ideas they came up with on their sticky notes in a useful and meaningful way (a concept map). This could involve putting reasons into categories and trying to find links between reasons. Ask some groups to feed back their ideas to the rest of the class. You may also like to record these on the board to add to at the end of the lesson.

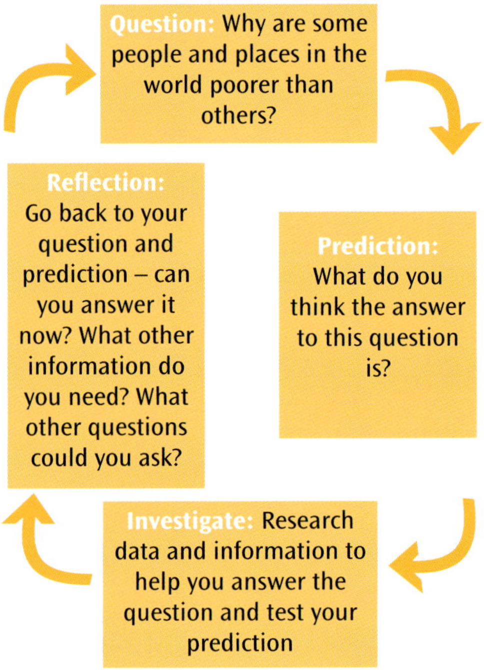

Figure 10: The independent enquiry cycle.

Main teaching phase
Display **Information Sheets 2-6** around the classroom (for large classes, make two copies to display). The Information Sheets refer to the following factors that can inhibit or stimulate the development of a country:
- Bolivia – youthful population, small but growing population
- India – literacy rates, natural resources, tourism, infrastructure, corruption
- Myanmar – topography, colonial past
- DR Congo – conflict, minerals, low wages
- South Africa – disease (HIV/AIDS), transport links, tourism.

Students must travel around the classroom and record key information from the Information Sheets to help them answer the enquiry question. They could use mini-whiteboards for this note-taking activity. Higher-attaining students should be encouraged to take their

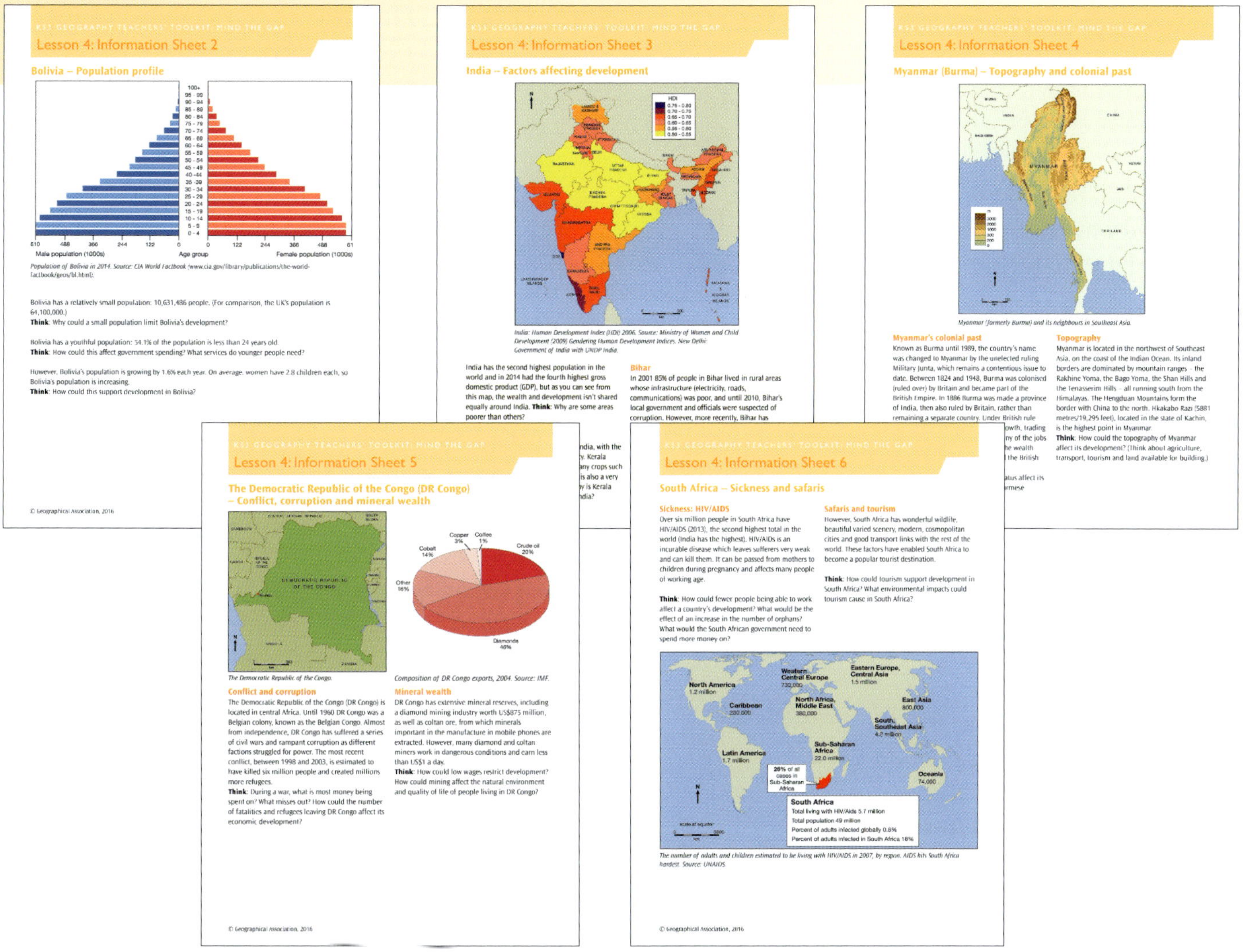

understanding further by answering the 'Think' questions on each Information Sheet as they make their notes.

You might like to designate roles within each group, to cater for different abilities and to ensure that all students take an active role. For example, one or two students could act as research envoys and make notes from the information around the classroom; the most able student could use a computer to carry out additional internet research; one student could be the co-ordinator, collecting information from the others and collating it on the group's A3 concept map.

Plenary

Students return to their groups, share their findings and add more information to their concept maps. Encourage them to include specific pieces of information they have learnt about the different countries (you may like them to do this in a different colour to illustrate progress). To challenge students further, ask them to find links between factors and explain how factors can inhibit or stimulate development. You might like to display the sample 'What a Good One Looks Like' (**PowerPoint 4, slide 2**) to support and stretch students. Revisit the enquiry question 'Why are some people and places in the world poorer than others?', asking some students to use their concept map to answer it.

Extension or homework activity

Students write up their reflections on their independent enquiry during the lesson. How would they answer the question now? What other information did they need? What other questions could they ask?

Teaching tips

Encouraging students to come up with their own categories for factors that inhibit/stimulate development promotes thinking skills, as well as team work.

WAGOLLs (What a good one looks like) model your expectations, which both supports and stretches students. You could also use a WABOLL (What a bad one looks like) to invite students to find errors in/improve a piece of work.

LESSON 5: Changing development

Key question

- How and why has Southeast Asia's development changed over time?

Learning objective

- To investigate how and why Southeast Asia's development has changed over time

Key words

- Transnational Corporations (TNCs)
- Gross Domestic Product (GDP)

Resources

- Activity sheet 8: Student task sheet and table
- Atlases
- Information sheet 7
- PowerPoint 5
- www.gapminder.org

Assessment opportunities

- Students describe and explain how development in Southeast Asia has changed over time in a short news item.

Starter

Students must guess the case study location for this and subsequent lessons using a series of up to ten clues. Show **PowerPoint 5**, **slide 2** (click on the slide to reveal each clue), or read from Figure 11. You might like to ask students to write down their answers on a mini-whiteboard when they have worked out the location and reward the students who needed the least clues. Provide students with atlases or refer them to **PowerPoint 5**, **slide 3**, and ask them to write a location description for Southeast Asia to improve their place knowledge.

1. This region is made up of 11 different countries.
2. Some parts of this region experience lots of earthquakes and volcanic eruptions.
3. There are 20,000 islands in this region.
4. Most of this region has a tropical climate (hot and humid all year around).
5. In this region you will find orang-utans, leopards, elephants, water buffalos and rhinos. Unfortunately, many of these animals are endangered.
6. The rainforest in this region is the second largest on Earth.
7. This region is facing severe deforestation. It is predicted that more than 40% of the animals and plant species here could be wiped out during the 21st century.
8. A lot of rice and rubber is grown in this region.
9. This region lies to the south/southeast of China.
10. This region lies to the northwest of Australia.

Figure 11: Clues to case study location.

Main teaching phase

Students can work independently or in pairs to carry out research into the development of a Southeast Asian country using *www.gapminder.org*. At the end of the lesson students share their findings with the rest of the class. Note that of Southeast Asian countries only Indonesia, Singapore, Malaysia, Thailand and the Philippines have full data sets, so restrict students to these five countries.

Hand out **Activity Sheet 8** – step-by-step instructions for navigating the Gapminder website. It would be useful to familiarise yourself with this before the lesson and to

explain to students how to manipulate the data and interpret the graph before they begin the research task. Students should work through each step and complete the table on **Activity Sheet 8**. They begin by researching how life expectancy, GDP/capita and the literacy rate have changed over time before choosing their own development indicators to research. To challenge students, encourage them to explain these changes. **Information Sheet 7** outlines the impact of globalisation and TNCs on the development of some of these countries. This should help students complete the final column of their table and explain the impact of the changes on the development of their country.

Students should share their findings in small groups or during a class discussion. How has development changed in their country over time? What evidence have they got to support this? How reliable is this data? Why has this region's development been so rapid? How might development change in the future?

Plenary

Students should now consolidate their understanding of development in Southeast Asia, using the following differentiated success criteria below (see also **PowerPoint 5**, **slide 4**):

- create a two-minute news item to describe how the development of your Southeast Asian country has changed over time, or
- compare your country's development with that of others in Southeast Asia, or
- explain why the development of your country has changed over time and what you think might happen in the future

You may like to set up a news desk at the front of the classroom and play the BBC News theme for students to present their news item to the rest of the class.

Extension or homework activity

Students think about their connections with countries in Southeast Asia and what they already know about them. Suggest that they look at the labels on their clothes, food or electronic items, or find source/manufacturing information for their films, music or holidays. Then they can create a collage or mindmap to summarise their connections and what they know about these places.

Teaching tip

To encourage students to extend their answers pose the question 'So what?' for them to answer at the end of each sentence.

LESSON 6: Equal development?

Key question
- How equal is development in Southeast Asia?

Learning objective
- To investigate how development varies across Southeast Asia

Key words
- Fairtrade
- Informal housing/shanty town
- Remittances
- Rural
- Trade
- Urban

Resources
- Activity Sheet 9: Role play cards
- Activity Sheet 10: Human development and inequality in Southeast Asia
- Atlases
- PowerPoint 6

Assessment opportunities
- Students write diary entries to describe and explain the lifestyles of people in different income groups across Southeast Asia
- Students summarise how equal they believe development is throughout Southeast Asia and why inequalities exist

Before the lesson
Before the lesson begins cut up the role play cards (**Activity Sheet 9**) and organise the desks so students can sit in groups of six.

Starter
Give each group a set of six cards (one x high income, two x middle income and three x low income) and an atlas. Note: The role play cards are differentiated, so allocate them to different students accordingly (high attainers – Ahmad, Danilo; middle attainers – Harmony, Rangsey, Vong; low attainers – Diah). If you have additional students, two students can play the same role within a group, but they should work independently.

Each student should read their role play card and locate the country they live in in the atlas. They should then introduce themselves to the rest of the group, using the information on their role play card. Explain to students that they represent real people who all have different lifestyles and income levels. Ask all students with a blue card to stand and explain that they are in the low income group. They represent the poorest people in the world and live on approximately 60p a day. Then, ask the students with a green card to stand. They represent the middle income group and live on approximately £6 a day. Finally, ask the students with red cards to stand. They represent the high income group, living on approximately £60 a day. Students should notice that there are a lot more people around the world living on 60p a day than on £60 a day. What does this suggest about development around the world? Where do you think people in the UK would fit? What do these figures mean for a person's quality of life? Interesting facts to share with students include:
- the average salary in the UK is £27,000 a year, which is nearly £74 a day
- in 2015, 80 individual people had a combined wealth equal to that of half of the world's population, while nearly a billion people struggled to feed their families.

Main teaching phase
Throughout the lesson students will compile a diary entry based on the life of the character on their role play card. They should write about:
- their family and social life
- their livelihood (e.g. job, money)
- the challenges they face
- their achievements/successes
- their feelings.

Students should be encouraged to use their imaginations and to empathise with their characters as well as use key geographical vocabulary. As the lesson continues, use **PowerPoint 6** to show each newsflash in turn (you might like to play a sound bite alongside the newsflash to get the students' attention). Each newsflash acts as a 'spanner in the works' and requires students to adapt their diary entry to take into account the changes in their character's life. To stretch students, you could ask them to answer the 'thinks' questions on each newsflash in their diary entry.

Plenary

Now, hand out **Activity Sheet 10** to pairs of students. This activity aims to consolidate and stretch learning from the previous activity and prepare students for the plenary. Ask students to annotate Map 1 to identify:

- the most developed country in Southeast Asia
- the least developed country in Southeast Asia.

Ask them to annotate Map 2 to identify:

- the most equal country in Southeast Asia
- the least equal country in Southeast Asia.

Students should attempt to explain why some countries are more developed/more equal than others, using their diary entry to help them. An interesting discussion point would be to ask students why Malaysia has a higher HDI than most Southeast Asian countries but also the highest inequality.

Students should now work as a group to answer two questions:

- How equal is development throughout Southeast Asia? (Think: Where/who are the wealthy people? Where and who are the poorer people?)
- Why does development vary throughout Southeast Asia? (Think: rural v urban, TNCs, Fairtrade, disease, education, resource use, remittances, climate, trade, human/work rights, gender)

Encourage all groups of students to share their points of view based on their role play character during the lesson. They should attempt to use key geographical terms and real examples from their diary entries in their answers. One person from each group should share their answers to the two questions with the rest of the class.

Extension or homework activity

Students should now reflect on their own home town, city, region or country and research how equal it is. This could be used as an extended homework activity or assessment requiring students to carry out their own research and submit a report or presentation of their findings. Students could use census and crime data to research household income, school exam results, incidences of crime, percentage unemployed and house prices.

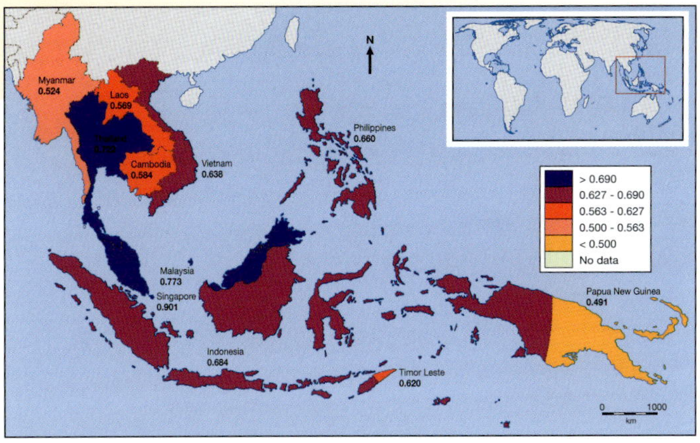

HDI levels worldwide in 1995.
Source: http://hdr.undp.org/ en/data/map.

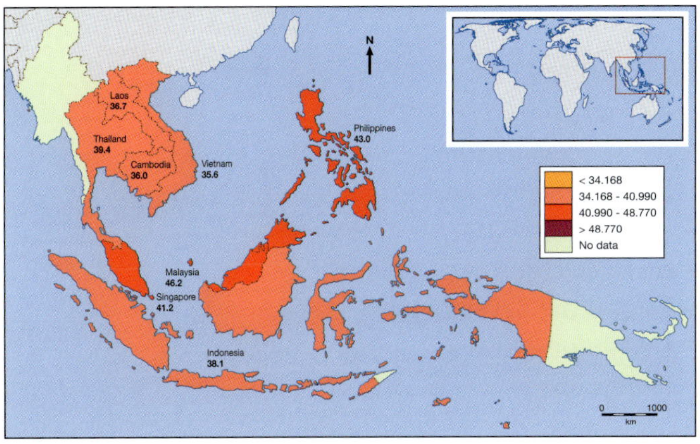

HDI levels worldwide in 2013.
Source: http://hdr.undp.org/ en/data/map.

Teaching tips

A diary entry is an extended piece of writing that can reinforce literacy skills and help students to empathise with people around the world. Beware: students may fall into the trap of stereotyping different people and cultures in this activity. Encourage students to recognise similarities as well as differences between them and their role play character (e.g. family relationships, hobbies, aspirations).

Make sure your, and your students', understanding of development is up to date, as the simplistic 'poor v rich countries' model does not apply to the 21st century. It is important to help students understand disparities in development within countries and to recognise Southeast Asia's rapid development. Hans Rosling has created a fantastic video which debunks the 'third world' myth, at *www.gapminder.org/videos/ted-talks/hans-rosling-ted-2006-debunking-myths-about-the-third-world*

Putting a 'spanner in the works' during a lesson can maintain students' engagement, encourage them to think outside the box and challenge them to respond to new information.

LESSON 7: The scale of development

Key question

- What is the difference between large-scale and small-scale development?
- How effective are large-scale approaches to development?

Learning objective

- To explore the roles of large-scale and small-scale approaches to development

Key words

- Air pollution
- Bio-sand water filter
- Export
- Habitat
- Hydroelectric power (HEP)
- Large-scale development
- Livelihood
- Renewable

Resources

- Activity Sheet 11: How effective are large-scale approaches to development?
- Information Sheet 8: Spot the differences
- Information Sheet 9: The Xayaburi Dam – Development or destruction?
- PowerPoint 7

Assessment opportunities

- Students use geographical thinking hats to evaluate the Xayaburi Dam project
- Students play 'argument tennis' to demonstrate the advantages and disadvantages of a large-scale approach to development

Starter

Display **PowerPoint 7**, **slide 2**, showing two photographs – the Xayaburi Hydroelectric Dam in Laos and a bio-sand water filter installed in Cambodia by the Trailblazer Foundation. Students should list as many differences they can think of between the two photographs. You may need to use 'Think' questions to guide students' thinking (see also **PowerPoint 7**, **slide 3**):

- How many people will benefit from each project?
- How much money will each project cost?
- How much technology is involved in each project?
- Who is in charge of each project?

Use **Information Sheet 8** to explain the differences between these two projects. Students should now be familiar with the meaning of small-scale and large-scale approaches to development. This lesson will go on to evaluate the large-scale Xayaburi Dam project.

Main teaching phase

Hand out **Activity Sheet 11** and **Information Sheet 9**. Students must read **Information Sheet 9** carefully, then evaluate the effectiveness of the Xayaburi Dam, working their way through **Activity Sheet 11** by 'wearing' each of the geographical thinking hats. Alternatively, you could ask students to work in a group of five, each taking a different 'thinking hat' and then debating as a group how effective large-scale approaches to development are. Stretch more able students by encouraging them to answer the question 'so what?' using key geographical terms (in bold type on **Information Sheet 9**). Finally, discuss with students the value of using different thinking hats in geography to evaluate a geographical issue.

Students now work in pairs to play 'argument tennis'. Number students one and two in their pairs, with number one arguing for large-scale development projects, such as the Xayaburi Dam, and number two arguing against them. Student one starts by 'serving' a reason supporting such projects, e.g. HEP dams provide renewable energy. Student two then 'returns' a reason against, e.g. 2100 people will have to move house because of the Xayaburi Dam. The student who is unable to 'return' a statement loses the 'point'. Students can call a 'fault' on their opponent if they believe the statement they use is incorrect/too vague; in this case the teacher acts as umpire. Students should note their 'serve' reasons and record the outcome for each one (returned/fault/ace/point lost/point won). If you have time you could ask students to swap roles within their pairs and take on the alternative viewpoint (i.e. number ones become number twos and vice versa). Encourage students to be specific and use key terms in their points.

Photo © The Stimson Center.

An example of a 'top down' development: Xayaburi Hydroelectric Dam, Laos.

Plenary

As a whole class, discuss all the 'ace' points and see if any other students have a 'return' for them. Record those that make it through this round as 'aces' and discuss why they are aces.

Extension or homework activity

Students carry out some online research on other large dam projects around the world. They could name five more dams and the countries where they are found, together with any other interesting information, such as the cost or number of people who had to be relocated.

Teaching tips

Geographical thinking hats encourage students to critically consider an issue from a range of perspectives and angles. They can be used to explore a range of geographical issues, such as deforestation, renewable vs non-renewable energies or coastal management strategies.

Argument tennis helps students to consolidate their understanding, provides an opportunity for peer teaching and supports oral literacy. Another oral plenary game is 'just a minute' where a student must talk about the issue, concept or case study they have learnt about for a minute without hesitation or repetition. If students work in pairs they can check each other's understanding and award points for the key geographical terms which have been used.

LESSON 8: Cost-effective development?

Key questions
- How effective are small-scale development projects?

Learning objective
- To explore the role of small-scale development projects

Key words
- Community
- Cost-benefit analysis
- Irrigation
- Non-governmental organisation (NGO)
- Small-scale development

Resources
- Activity Sheet 12: Role play cards for Siem Reap hot-seating activity
- Activity Sheet 13: How effective are small-scale approaches to development?
- Activity Sheet 14: Cost-benefit analysis
- Activity Sheet 15: Researching development projects
- PowerPoint 8

Assessment opportunities
- Students evaluate small- and large-scale approaches to development by carrying out a cost-benefit analysis of two projects

Prior to the lesson
Choose five students to become actors; they will each take on the role of a different stakeholder involved in the Trailblazer Foundation's work and will be 'hot-seated' (asked questions) during the lesson. You could ask the drama teacher to nominate students for this role.

Starter
Ask students to write down all the ways they have used water since getting out of bed (you could show **PowerPoint 8**, **slide 2**). They also need to think about ways in which water has been/is involved in wider aspects of their morning routine: you could reward students for coming up with the least obvious use of water (e.g. in a car, in radiators, growing cotton to make their clothes) to encourage them to think beyond drinks and washing. After discussing numerous uses, ask students to consider how their life would be different if they didn't have access to clean water from a tap in their house (**PowerPoint 8**, **slide 3**). Who would have to collect water? How could this affect their life? What would happen if you or your parents got poorly? What would you have to do to water before using it?

Main teaching phase
Introduce students to Siem Reap province, Cambodia – the case study location for this lesson – using **PowerPoint 8**, **slide 4**. Explain to students that the poverty line is US$2 a day (approximately £1.30). To put this figure in context, compare this to how much students spend each day and what they spend it on. Now use slide 5 to introduce students to the Trailblazer Foundation, a real non-governmental organisation (NGO). It explains the aims of the Trailblazer Foundation: to use small-scale and community-based approaches to development to provide clean water to rural areas of Siem Reap.

Hand out one role play card from **Activity Sheet 12** to each of the five 'actor' students. The actors have three minutes to read the information on their role play card and complete the middle column of **Activity Sheet 13** by answering the 'Think' questions on their card. Simultaneously, the rest of the class will become 'development detectives' and have three minutes to come up with three questions, using **Activity Sheet 13**, which asks them to evaluate small-scale development projects.

Plenary
Students carry out a cost-benefit analysis (**Activity Sheet 14**) of large-scale and small-scale development projects. You may like to start by leading a class discussion about both approaches to development to refresh students' understanding from Lesson 7. Which is most expensive? Which has the greatest impact on people? Which has the greatest impact on the environment? What are the disadvantages of each approach? Students come to a final verdict and explain which approach they believe is most effective for development. More able students should show understanding that both approaches have their advantages and disadvantages and appreciate the relevance of the context where each development approach is being used.

Photos top left and right © Michelle Minton.

Extension

Using **Activity Sheet 15**, groups of three or four students research one of a selection of development projects and answer a set of questions about it.

Teaching tips

Asking students to generate questions instead of answering them encourages enquiry and research skills. To support students with this task encourage them to use the 5Ws (What, Where, When, Why and Who).

The Trailblazer Foundation is a real NGO working with real people in Siem Reap, Cambodia. The role play characters are all real and reflect the work of the Trailblazer Foundation. Encourage students to keep this in mind during the course of the lesson.

Photos bottom left and right © The Trailblazer Foundation.

LESSON 9: Supporting development

Key questions
- How can countries work together to support development?

Learning objective
- To explore global approaches to development

Key words
- Child mortality
- Environmental sustainability
- Gender equality
- Millennium Development Goals (MDGs)
- Poverty
- United Nations (UN)

Resources
- Activity Sheet 16: MDG facts and figures
- PowerPoint 9

Assessment opportunities
- Students write a PEE chain paragraph to explain why they think the MDGs have been successful or not
- Students work in groups of four to write a campaign speech advocating a new goal for global development

Starter
Display **PowerPoint 9**, **slide 2** and ask students to come up with three goals in their life, using SMART to make sure the goals are Specific, Measurable, Achievable, Relevant and Timely. You can use this opportunity to ask students to consider what is most important to them (e.g. friends, family, happiness, careers, sport) and make links between this and the meaning of 'development'. You might also like to ask students to think about different time frames, e.g. goals for 10 years, 20 years and 30 years.

Main teaching phase
Show students the United Nations logo on slide 3 and ask them to consider what is represents – why is there a circle? What leaf/branch is shown? Why? Why is there a map? Tell them that it is the logo of the United Nations (UN) and ask students what they already know about this organisation. Now show slide 4, a brief history of the UN and its role in peacekeeping and global development. Students may have heard of the United Nations International Children's Emergency Fund (UNICEF) and know of famous ambassadors such as David Beckham and Angelina Jolie. Introduce students to the 2000–2015 Millennium Development Goals (MDGs) and ask them to predict what worldwide problems they aimed to solve. Continue the explanation and discussion of the MDGs using slide 5 – how many goals did they guess? Did any of the goals surprise them? How effective do they think they have been, considering what they have learnt in previous lessons?

Give pairs of students a set of cards (**Activity Sheet 16**), which includes facts about the MDGs. Students should sort these cards into categories; to encourage thinking skills avoid telling students the categories. They are likely to sort the cards into successes and shortcomings. Follow the card sort with a class discussion as some cards could be categorised differently depending on the angle students take.

Students now work independently to write a PEE chain paragraph to explain whether they believe the Millennium Development Goals were successful or not. Use the WAGOLL (What a good one looks like) on slide 6 to model a PEE chain paragraph to students.

Plenary

Finish the lesson by asking the class to democratically decide on three new global development goals for the next 15 years to suggest to the UN. Split students into groups of four; each group comes up with one goal they believe is most important for global development and writes a one-minute campaign speech to advocate this goal to the rest of the class, using the success criteria on **PowerPoint 9**, **slide 7**. Write each proposed goal on the whiteboard. After all groups have delivered their campaign speeches, each student has three votes to choose the three goals to put forward to the UN. Then, show them the Global Goals for Sustainable Development for 2015-2030. How do these goals compare with the ones they proposed?

Extension or homework activity

Students choose the three Global Goals for Sustainable Development they think are most important and argue the case for making these three goals a priority. How do their three choices compare with the three goals voted for by the whole class during the plenary?

Teaching tips

SMART can also be used for self- and peer-assessment when setting targets for improvement.

PEE (point, evidence, explain) is a useful literacy strategy to support students in structuring a paragraph as well as stretch them to explain their points in detail using connectives.

P – Students make a **point**, a simple sentence which summarises their opinion

E – Students add **evidence** to support their point; this should facts, figures or case study information

E – Students **explain** their evidence and opinion. Prompt students by asking them the question 'So what?' and encourage them to start this sentence with a connective.

For more able students you could add an L (for 'Link'): this requires them to link ideas together or make a comparison with an alternative point of view.

LESSON 10: Development roles

Key questions

- Whose responsibility is development and do we have a role to play?

Learning objective

- To investigate the role of different stakeholders in development

Key words

- Consumers
- Stakeholder

Resources

- Activity Sheet 17: Who is responsible for the situations shown in these images?
- Activity Sheet 18: Who is responsible for development?
- Activity Sheet 19: Progress questionnaire: What do you think about international development now?
- PowerPoint 10

Assessment opportunities

- Students discuss the responsibility of different stakeholders in development
- Students write a citizenship charter that consolidates understanding from this unit of work
- A comparison of students' answers to the baseline questionnaire and the progress questionnaire

Starter

Give each pair of students one of the six photographs from **Activity Sheet 17**. Allocate the starvation photo to the least able students, and air pollution in China to the most able. They should study their photograph carefully and consider who is responsible for the situation shown. Pairs should share their thoughts with the rest of the class.

Main teaching phase

Give pairs of students **Activity Sheet 18**, which sets out eight different views of the possible role of stakeholders in development. Stakeholders include rich countries, the UN, TNCs, consumers, governments in LDCs, charities and NGOs, communities in LDCs and journalists. Students read through the statements, answer the 'Think' questions on each card, decide which stakeholder they believe holds the greatest responsibility for development and then justify their choice in a class discussion.

Now, students should return to the photograph they were given at the beginning of the lesson and consider how they could respond to the situations shown. For example, they could donate money/clothes/food to charity, boycott TNCs that use sweatshops, advocate green energy, volunteer for a homeless charity in the UK, campaign on issues or buy Fairtrade products. This activity aims to encourage students to become active citizens and recognise that they can have a role in development. More able students should critically consider such actions. For example, is buying Fairtrade honey from Mexico better than buying local honey from the UK? How much of the money you donate to charity reaches the people who need it most? Why could donating clothes to India create a problem for the local seamstresses? Is tourism really benefitting local communities in Cambodia or is it eroding their culture?

Plenary

To consolidate understanding from this unit of work students should write their own citizenship charter to support development in the UK and around the world using the success criteria shown in Figure 12 and **PowerPoint 10**, **slide 2**. Students may come up with ideas such as buying Fairtrade, recycling, voting,

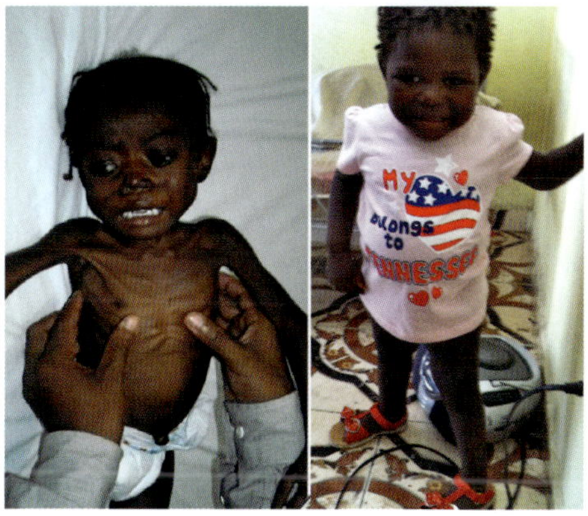

Photo © Cuddly Little Owl.

Photo © Feed My Starving Children.

Photo © Aon_Skynotlimit Shutterstock.

Photo © Institute for Global Labour and Human Rights.

volunteering and campaigning. This piece of work would make a fantastic display around school and could be linked to a 'school citizenship charter'.

To measure attitudinal change and learning throughout this unit you could also use **Activity Sheet 19** and compare with the baseline questionnaire completed at the beginning of the unit.

It must:

- include at least five guidelines for how individuals can support development in the UK and around the world.

It should:

- include practical examples and advice, e.g. weblinks, names of ethical companies
- use persuasive language effectively.

It could:

- explain how each guideline will support development in the UK and around the world
- find links between our roles and those of other stakeholders in development.

Figure 12: Citizenship Charter success criteria.

Teaching tips

You could use lollipop sticks to ensure all students take part in class discussions, as quieter students can often be overlooked.

- Option 1 – write down all the students' names on lollipop sticks and use these to randomly pick students to question.
- Option 2 – give each student a lollipop stick at the beginning of the lesson. Place a cup in the middle of each table; once students have given an answer they can put their lollipop stick into the cup on the table. You could challenge more able students by giving them more lollipop sticks.

GLOSSARY

accessibility – how easy or difficult it is to get to a location

air pollution – harmful substances, e.g. carbon dioxide emissions, in the atmosphere

bio-sand water filter – a simple household water treatment device that filters the water through sand to remove up to 90% of bacteria and 100% of parasites

child mortality – the number of children who die before they are five years old

choropleth map – a map on which areas are coloured or shaded to show the proportion in that area of the statistic being mapped

colonialism – the policy of acquiring other countries to rule as colonies

community – a group of people living in the same place

conflict – a disagreement or argument; can also refer to war

consumer – a person who buys or uses something

cost-benefit analysis – to assess something by weighing up the benefits against the costs

development – the use of human and physical resources to improve standards of living

development indicator – a statistic used to measure a country's development

environmental sustainability – looking after the natural world, for the present and the future

export – send something out of a country, usually to be sold

Fairtrade – trade where fair prices are paid, usually by MDCs for goods, made in LDCs

gender equality – men and women having the same rights and opportunities

gross domestic product (GDP) – the sum total of goods and services produced by a country in a given year (usually in US dollars)

gross domestic product per capita (GDP/capita) – as above, divided by the total number of people in the country

habitat – where a plant or animal lives

Human Development Index (HDI) – a way of measuring a country's development, scoring from 0.000 to 1

Hydroelectric power (HEP) – energy produced by water moving through turbines

infant mortality rate – the number of babies per 1000 born who die before their first birthday

informal housing – illegal housing usually built on marginal lands, e.g. on hillsides, alongside train tracks

infrastructure – communication links and utilities, e.g. roads, electricity

irrigation – the watering of crops

large-scale development – large development projects, usually driven by government or business

LDC – less developed country

life expectancy – the average age a person is likely to reach

literacy rate – the percentage of people aged 15 and over who can read and write

livelihood – the way people support themselves, e.g. to get money, food, shelter

Millennium Development Goals (MDGs) – a set of eight development targets set by the UN in 2000

MDC – more developed country

NIC – newly industrialised country

Non-governmental organisation (NGO) – a non-profit voluntary group that is not part of a government, e.g. Oxfam

poverty – a lack of money and other resources

poverty line – the minimum level of money needed to survive in a particular country

remittances – money earned then gifted to other people, e.g. city workers sending money to family in the countryside

renewable – a resource that will not run out

rural – in the country

shanty town – an area of informal housing, usually on the edge of a city

small-scale development – small, community-driven development projects

stakeholder – a person/organisation involved in or affected by development

topography – the shape of the landscape

trade – buying and selling goods and services

transnational corporation (TNC) – a business that operates in more than one country

United Nations (UN) – a global organisation to promote international co-operation

urban – a city/built up area

youthful population – a population with a high proportion of young people

FURTHER SOURCES FOR IDEAS

Lesson 1: Defining development

Up-to-date videos dispelling myths about development can be found at *www.gapminder.org/videos*

Lesson 2: Measuring development

For more development statistics and indicators see *www.cia.gov/library/publications/resources/the-world-factbook/index.html* and *http://unstats.un.org/unsd/default.htm*

Lesson 3: Varying development

See *http://hdr.undp.org/en/content/human-development-index-hdi* for more HDI statistics and information. You could also visit *www.gapminder.org* or *www.worldmapper.org* for innovative graphs and maps showing development around the world.

Lesson 5: Changing development

www.gapminder.org should be used to investigate development over time in Southeast Asia.

Lesson 7: The scale of development

For more information about the Xayaburi Dam and the Mekong River Project see *http://peakwater.org/tag/xayaburi-dam*, *http://www.internationalrivers.org*, *www.oxfam.org.au/explore/infrastructure-people-and-environment/save-the-mekong/damming-the-mekong/xayaburi-dam* and *www.savethemekong.org*

Lesson 8: Cost-effective development?

For more information on the Trailblazer Foundation see *www.thetrailblazerfoundation.org*

Lesson 9: Supporting development

See *www.un.org/en/about-un* for more information about the history of the UN, and *www.unmillenniumproject.org/goals* for additional information about the Millennium Development Goals. visit: See *https://sustainabledevelopment.un.org* and *www.undp.org/content/undp/en/home/mdgoverview.html* for information about the new sustainable development goals.

Photo © Bryan Ledgard.

References and further information

Adiche, C. (2009) *The dangers of a single story*. Available online at: www.ted.com/talks/chimamanda_adichie_the_danger_of_a_single_story.html (last accessed 2 September 2015).

BBC News (no date) *Manila Slum Life*. Available online at: http://news.bbc.co.uk/nol/shared/spl/hi/picture_gallery/06/world_manila_slum_life/print.stm (last accessed 2 September 2015).

Claire, H. and Holden, C. (2007) *The Challenge of Teaching Controversial issues*. London: Trentham Books.

Diamond, J. (1997) *Guns, Germs and Steel*. New York, NY: Norton and Co.

Lambert, D. and Morgan, J. (2011) *Geography and Development: Development education in schools and the part played by geography teachers*. London: Development Education Research Centre.

Leeds Development Education Centre (Leeds DEC) (2012) *The Global Teacher*. Leeds: DEC.

New Economics Foundation (2015) *Happy Planet Index*. Available online at: www.happyplanetindex.org (last accessed 2 September 2015).

Rosling, H. (2013) *The River of Myths*. Available online at: www.gapminder.org/videos/the-river-of-myths (last accessed 2 September 2015).

Stradling, R. (1985) 'Controversial issues in the curriculum', *Bulletin of Environmental Education*, 170, pp. 9–13.

UN Development Programme (2015) *Human Development Index*. Available online at: http://hdr.undp.org/en/content/human-development-index-hdi) (last accessed 2 September 2015).

ASSESSMENT FRAMEWORK

Students should be expected to make progress throughout their key stage 3 geography programme and within each unit of work. Of course, the starting and finishing point (what were previously described as 'levels' in the geography National Curriculum) will differ for each student. Rates of progress will also differ.

In the diagram below, student progression is measured in three broad bands – what might previously have been described as 'levels'. These bands are:

- most students at key stage 3 (previously levels 5-6)
- students who progress at a slower rate (previously levels 3-4)
- students who progress at a faster rate (previously levels 7-8).

The diagram describes the learning outcomes for students in each of the three bands.

Students who progress at a slower rate:

- show some understanding of the term 'development' and describe ways it can be measured
- describe simply how a number of factors can influence development around the world
- identify and describe differences between small- and large-scale approaches to development
- identify a range of Millennium Development Goals and describe their role
- identify and begin to describe the role different stakeholders can play in development
- interpret atlas maps to identify countries and major cities.

Most students at KS3:

- define the term development and apply the terms MDC, LDC and NIC to different countries using development indicators
- explain how factors can influence development around the world and within a country using some examples
- explain the costs and benefits of large-scale and small-scale approaches to development
- describe and begin to explain the costs and benefits of the Millennium Development Goals and global approaches to development in general
- explain the role different stakeholders play in development using examples
- interpret atlas maps, graphs and development indicators to explore the development of different countries.

Students who progress at a faster rate:

- critically assess countries' development using a range of development indicators
- explore links between factors that influence development around the world and within countries
- critically evaluate large- and small-scale approaches to development using named examples as evidence
- evaluate the success of the Millennium Development Goals using evidence
- assess the responsibility of different stakeholders in development and explore their own role in development
- use a wide range of resources, including atlas maps, graphs, development indicators and choropleth maps, to research development of different countries now and in the future.